Kenny Emson

The Shit

T0161534

Salamander Street

PLAYS

First published in 2022 by Salamander Street Ltd.
(info@salamanderstreet.com)

The Shit © Kenny Emson, 2022

ISBN: 9781914228650

10 9 8 7 6 5 4 3 2 1

CAST

SARA *(Voice)* Samantha Béart

ERIC Lladel Bryant

DANIEL Dillon Scott-Lewis

CREATIVE TEAM

Writer Kenny Emson

Director Alexander Ferris

Set and Costume Design Caitlin Mawhinney

Lighting Designer Ciarán Cunningham

Sound Designer DJ NikNak

Lighting Programmer Chris Speight

Assistant Director *(Leeds City College Placement)* Evie Luby

Assistant Support Worker Madeleine Wood

Workshop Leader Joseph Hancock

Producer Matthew Schmolle Productions

PRODUCTION TEAM

Production Manager Martyn Sands

Stage Manager Eve Machin

The Shit was first performed at Leeds Playhouse on 5 March 2022.

Supported by Arts Council England, The Spears-Stutz Charitable Trust, The Stage One Bursary Scheme, Leeds City College, Leeds Playhouse, AJS and JS.

Thanks to all the incredible workers and young people at PT, OC, Immediate, The City Hall Peer Outreach Team, Lewisham Youth First, Breeze Arts and Leeds City College.

Thanks also to the amazing staff at Leeds Playhouse for allowing us to make the show in the most supportive environment we could have hoped for.

Massive thanks to the incredible Sofie Mason, Diana Jervis-Read, Oliver Everett, Laura Gallo, Bernice Chitnis and Joachim Fleury of Off West End Plays and Playwrights for their continued support of mine and so many other writers' careers.

A debt of gratitude also to Craig, Vinnie, Cher, Muna, Eric, Omar and many, many others. Wherever you are and whatever you're doing we hope you are happy and healthy. Big love.

◎ THE **WORKING**PARTY

The Working Party make theatre to make change. TWP are a performing arts charity that design and deliver high quality projects, performances and creative acts through both commissioning and the traditional production process and by co-creating with identified communities in areas that rate high on the multiple indices of depravation and have limited access to the arts. TWP initiates its own work and, with its wealth of experience, produces and supports other artists it respects to create the socially impactful projects and performances they want to make.

T: @theworkingparty
I: @theworkingpartytc
F: @theworkingpartytc

Matthew Schmolle Productions independently produces critically acclaimed theatre and performance across mid-scale, studio, festival and fringe, nationally and internationally. It also produces and manages large scale public art projects and events.

T: @mattschprodsltd
I: @mattschprodsltd
F: @mattschprodsltd

ABOUT THE PROJECT

The modern story of youth work is not an easy one. It is a story of continual cuts, squeezed capacity and lack of understanding versus rising need and rising complexity. In early 2022 the YMCA published their DEVALUED report which, amongst much alarming news, revealed there has been a 74% or £1.1 billion fall in funding to youth services since 2010/11. At the centre of this are the young people and youth workers that form the heart of our show. In 2018 and 2019 we spent six months talking with, work-shopping with and interviewing young people and youth workers collectively and individually. All of the TWP project staff had previously worked closely with young people in front line work and were painfully aware of the difficulty and sometimes impossibility of working to create space in a system for people that have been side-lined by it. It is arduous, constant and infuriating work with some of the most vulnerable, traumatised and also inspiring people you can imagine. Boundaries are crossed, mistakes are made and the work, like the situation, is often less than perfect. But it is an under-funded fight against an almost unbeatable force bent on excluding some people from the chance of a full and realised life, so it was always going to be a bit messy.

Our intention with this piece is to start a conversation about an area of work that is too often over-looked and misunderstood and we think deserves a respect, support and acknowledgment that it does not currently receive.

For Ange

Cast

Eric – Late thirties.
*Black. Born in Yorkshire but lived in South London
long enough to not have a notable accent.*

Daniel – Seventeen.
White. North Londoner.

Sara – Late forties. Eric's supervisor.

Young Man

Nb.

The role of **Young Man** *should be played
by the same actor as* **Daniel.**

Author's Note.

Punctuation is used to mark delivery in performance not to conform to
the rules of grammar.

(/) means the next speech begins at that point.

(–) means the next line or thought interrupts what is currently being said.

(…) marks the trailing off of a line.

The community centre.

Two chairs. But maybe twenty. Maybe a hundred. A thousand. The more the room is full of them, the better.

ERIC *sits facing* **DANIEL.**

A long silence.

ERIC: Dizzy or Stormzy?

> *Pause.*

Grime or Bashment?

> *Pause.*

Skepta or Ed Sheeran?

> **DANIEL** *kisses his teeth.*

A noise. Well, now we're getting somewhere. McDonalds or KFC?

> *Pause.*

Come on, everyone has an opinion.

> *Pause.*

Coffee or tea?

DANIEL: You the refreshment lady?

ERIC: Can be. You thirsty?

DANIEL: Don't drink caffeine. Bad for you, innit.

ERIC: Coke?

DANIEL: You dumb or something?

ERIC: I ain't the one who came here and sat in silence for an hour.

> *Beat.*

DANIEL: Doesn't say I have to talk to get signed off.

ERIC: So this is your plan?

Another silence.

Smart. We can really get somewhere with that attitude.

DANIEL: Look, I've done this before. The last one. *Brian.* He done it all already. Fixed me. I'm motivated. Changed man, innit.

ERIC: You only saw him for two sessions.

DANIEL: He quit. Not me.

ERIC: He didn't quit.

DANIEL: Give a fuck.

ERIC: I know –

DANIEL: What do you know?

ERIC: I know it's not easy changing youth worker so early in a course of sessions.

DANIEL: Course? What is this, therapy yeah? You gonna therapise my brain? Make me better yeah?

ERIC: No, I –

DANIEL: *'Drink and drugs are bad. Committing crime is bad. You want to have a shit life? No? Better get yourself on the straight and narrow then, innit. This is your last chance. Can't fuck it up. Here's an application form to work in JD Sports…'.* That your speech? Yeah. Heard it already, bruv. And it was boring then. So sign the form and we can both fuck this waste of time off.

He checks his phone.

Time's up man. We're done. You gonna sign the form or what?

ERIC *takes a piece of paper and signs it.*

DANIEL *gets up and starts towards the exit.*

ERIC: Good talk.

A small office.

ERIC *sits with his supervisor,* **SARA**.

SARA: Communication?

ERIC: One.

SARA: Working with others?

ERIC: One.

SARA: Setting and achieving goals?

ERIC: One.

SARA: Confidence?

ERIC: Six.

SARA: Reliability?

ERIC: Five.

SARA: Leadership skills?

ERIC: One.

SARA: Managing feelings?

A beat…

3.

The community centre.

ERIC *and* **DANIEL** *sit on a different axis of the room. Or new chairs if there are more than two.*

In between them there are lots of sheets of paper laid out in a semi-circle.

ERIC: At least have a look.

Silence.

Think of all those trees that died so I could print them out.

DANIEL: Didn't ask you to print them out, did I?

ERIC: It's my job.

DANIEL: Nice job. You like a secretary or something, yeah? Mister printer man. Mister tea and coffee man. *(He kisses his teeth.)* Telling me about your big job. Jokes.

ERIC *picks up one of the sheets of paper.*

ERIC: Read it.

He places the paper on **DANIEL**'s *lap.*

Read. It.

A silence.

DANIEL *grabs the piece of paper, screws it up and throws it violently across the room.*

DANIEL: Fuck this, man.

DANIEL *stands.*

ERIC: Daniel.

DANIEL: You taking the piss, yeah? You think you're funny?

ERIC: I'm just trying to show you some –

DANIEL: You know, don't you? He told you.

ERIC: Know what?

DANIEL: Fuck this. You think I'm gonna come here just to be laughed at?

ERIC: I'm not laughing at you.

DANIEL: Yeah you are.

ERIC: How about you sit down and tell me what the problem is?

Pause.

DANIEL: I can't read.

Beat.

Big fucking joke, yeah? Ha fucking ha.

ERIC: I... I'm sorry. I didn't –

6

DANIEL: I told Brian. Said he understood. That he could help.

ERIC: I didn't know. I promise.

> **ERIC** *walks across the room. Collects the piece of paper that* **DANIEL** *launched. Comes back to his chair.*

I'll read them to you. It's alright. And I can refer you to a –

> **DANIEL** *starts laughing loudly.*

ERIC: What's funny?

DANIEL: You are. Just bait, yeah.

ERIC: Bait?

DANIEL: Course you think people like me can't read.

ERIC: I didn't –

DANIEL: Yeah you did. I see you. All of you.

> **DANIEL** *stretches out on the chair. Puts his hands behind his head.*

So you can keep your forms man. Keep your referrals too. Just tell me when it's time. That's what you can do for me mister secretary man.

4.

The office.

SARA: Confidence?

ERIC: Six.

SARA: Reliability?

ERIC: Five.

SARA: Leadership skills?

ERIC: One.

SARA: Managing feelings?

> *A beat…*

The community centre.

ERIC *and* **DANIEL** *sit on a different axis of the room.*

A silence.

ERIC *looks down at his watch.*

ERIC: Time.

> **DANIEL** *stands, slings a bag over his shoulders and starts towards the exit.*

DANIEL: Laters.

The office.

SARA: Managing feelings?

> *Pause.*

> Managing feelings?

> *A silence*

> Is there a problem?

ERIC: No.

SARA: You look tired, Eric.

ERIC: I've got twice as many clients.

SARA: There's not a lot I can do about that. / Cuts.

ERIC: *Cuts.*

SARA: I didn't want to have to let Brian go.

ERIC: But you did.

SARA: Do I look like I oversee government spending budgets?

ERIC: I didn't say that.

SARA: I'm not the bad guy.

ERIC: You just work for the bad guy.

SARA: We all work for the bad guy. That's life.

Beat.

How's the baby?

ERIC: A handful.

SARA: It's your first isn't it?

ERIC: Yeah.

SARA: Try and enjoy it.

ERIC: The late nights? Lack of sleep?

SARA: It doesn't last. Then you miss it. They're simple when they're that age.

Pause.

ERIC: Sara…

SARA: Yeah?

ERIC: My job's safe, right?

SARA: As safe as anyone's in the public sector.

ERIC: I've got responsibilities.

SARA: So did, Brian.

7.

The community centre.

ERIC and **DANIEL** *sit on a different axis of the room.*

DANIEL: Time?

    ERIC *looks at his watch. Nods. He stands up and starts off towards the door.*

Where you going?

ERIC: Home. Session's up.

DANIEL: But –

ERIC: *Laters.*

The office.

SARA: Communication?

ERIC: One.

SARA: Working with others?

ERIC: One.

SARA: Setting and achieving goals?

ERIC: One.

SARA: Confidence?

ERIC: Six.

SARA: Reliability?

ERIC: Six.

SARA: Leadership skills?

ERIC: One.

SARA: Managing feelings?

A beat…

The community centre.

ERIC *and* **DANIEL** *sit on a different axis of the room.*

A very long silence.

DANIEL: Proper chatty man, ain't you?

ERIC: Say the same about you.

DANIEL: Not my job.

ERIC: Not my job either.

DANIEL: Think you'll find actually it is, fam.

ERIC: You don't wanna talk, then we can just sit here.

DANIEL: Ark at you with the old reverse psychologising shit.

ERIC: Ain't *reverse pyschologising* nothing.

DANIEL: Lol. Course not.

Beat.

What's the time? We gotta be done by now. This is long.

ERIC: Do I look like the speaking clock?

DANIEL: What's a speaking clock?

ERIC *laughs.*

Something funny?

ERIC: Fuck, you're young.

DANIEL: What's that meant to mean?

ERIC: That you're a kid. Sometimes / I forget.

DANIEL: Wanna watch your mouth.

Beat.

Just sign the form man, then we can both get on with our lives.

ERIC: Hour's not up yet.

DANIEL: Who cares?

ERIC: I do.

DANIEL: Rah.

ERIC: Yeah. Rah.

Beat.

You wanna know a secret?

DANIEL: Better than just having you stare at me.

ERIC: Is that a yes?

DANIEL: *Yes.*

ERIC*:* I don't think you want me to just sign the form.

DANIEL: Nah?

ERIC: Think you're fronting.

DANIEL: *Fronting.* Look at you, mister bad man.

ERIC: Just thought I'd share my thoughts. Might make it easier for you. To admit it.

DANIEL: Yeah, fam. You got me.

Pause.

What am I fronting for then, mister clever suit and tie man?

ERIC: You want to talk.

DANIEL: Yeah. Course. Why I'm always conversationing with you, innit.

ERIC: *Conversationing* now, ain't you? Keep turning up here too. Sitting there, staring your stare.

DANIEL: Gotta turn up. Condition of my license seeing one of yous, innit.

ERIC: Nah, I reckon you wanna talk.

DANIEL: To a Fed?

ERIC *starts laughing.*

Am I a fucking comedian or something?

ERIC: I'm not a Fed.

DANIEL: Might as well be.

ERIC: I'm here to try and –

DANIEL: Look like a Fed.

ERIC: Really?

DANIEL: Yeah. Proper desk Fed. Suit and tie Fed. Not got the arms to be a real Fed, Fed.

ERIC: My arms are in pretty good shape.

DANIEL: Psht. What can you bench?

ERIC: Don't believe in gyms

DANIEL: They ain't the fucking tooth fairy.

ERIC: Naturally toned.

DANIEL: Fat people say stuff like that. Get yourself some weights, bro. Male obesity's a killer. Especially at your age.

ERIC: I'm touched by your concern.

DANIEL: No dramas. Mister small arm Fed, man.

ERIC: Mind if I ask you a question, while we're getting on so well.

DANIEL: Say what you want.

ERIC: As you hate the Feds so much, how come you keep spending so much time with them?

DANIEL: What you saying?

ERIC: Just an observation.

DANIEL: Don't need no observations. Need you to sort out getting me moved outta my house. How many times I gotta ask?

Beat.

ERIC: What?

DANIEL: You cunts not speak to each other when you pass us on?

ERIC: Can you not call me a cu –

DANIEL: Brian. Told him I wanted to get out of my dad's place. The area. Fresh start, innit. He said he'd make some calls for me. Get me on the council list.

ERIC: Okay, well I can look into that for you.

DANIEL: What he said and all.

ERIC *makes a note of this.*

ERIC: Why didn't you mention this before?

DANIEL: Why should I?

ERIC: Well, I enjoy our staring competitions as much as the next man, but this is actually something we can –

DANIEL: Ain't a competition.

ERIC: If it was, I'm definitely winning.

DANIEL: Whatever.

Pause.

ERIC: I can help you, Daniel. You just have to let me.

DANIEL: I look like a charity case or something?

ERIC: I wasn't –

DANIEL: DO I LOOK LIKE A FUCKING CHARITY CASE?

Beat.

You think I need your fucking help? Look at the state of you. Help yourself.

A silence.

ERIC: So we'll just sit here then? Like normal?

DANIEL: Good for me.

10.

The office.

SARA: Reliability?

ERIC: Six.

SARA: Leadership skills?

ERIC: One.

SARA: Managing feel –

ERIC: Daniel mentioned trying to get out of the area.

SARA: Can we finish this before we –

ERIC: That he'd asked Brian to get him on the council register.

SARA: And?

ERIC: None of that was in my notes when I took him on.

SARA: Because it isn't going to happen.

ERIC: He said Brian –

SARA: Is he in danger? Is he homeless?

ERIC: No, but –

SARA: Tell him you'll refer it to YOS. The priority is getting him back into employment. You know that.

ERIC: How is he ever going to trust me if the one thing he asks for help with, I just pass over to someone else?

SARA: Don't bring it up then. See if he forgets.

ERIC: I really don't think that's –

SARA: Of course he wants his own place. Somewhere he can bring a girl back to. Somewhere he can get stoned all day.

ERIC: That wasn't what he was saying.

SARA: Read between the lines.

Beat.

Look, Eric, help him with what you can help him with. Don't make promises you can't keep.

11.

The community centre.

ERIC *and* **DANIEL** *sit on a different axis of the room.*

DANIEL *stands, moves his chair much closer to* **ERIC***. Sits back down.*

ERIC *doesn't flinch. Holds his stare. Their faces are now almost touching.*

DANIEL *takes out a cigarette.*

ERIC: Can't smoke in here.

DANIEL: Says who?

ERIC: Says me.

DANIEL: Look at you, mister-man. Mister-rule-man. Worried you're gonna get in shit, mister-rule-man? Is that it?

ERIC: I'm worried about you getting cancer.

DANIEL: Everyone's gotta die from something.

> **DANIEL** *kisses his teeth. Puts the cigarette back into the packet. Pulls out a Vape and starts to smoke that.*

ERIC: You taking the piss?

DANIEL: What?

ERIC: Ain't they meant to help you give up the fags?

DANIEL: Indoor smoking, innit. As I can't do my real smoking.

> *He lets out a large plume of vape.* **ERIC** *coughs.*

You not got the lungs for it, fam.

ERIC: What is that, blueberry?

DANIEL: Paradise.

ERIC: The flavour.

DANIEL: That's what I just told you.

ERIC: Paradise ain't a flavour.

DANIEL: Paradise is whatever you want it to be.

> *Pause.*

ERIC: Let me have a go.

> **DANIEL** *kisses his teeth.*

What?

DANIEL: As if I'm gonna let you touch my vape.

ERIC: Why not?

DANIEL: Don't know where you've been, do I?

ERIC: You want a doctor's note?

DANIEL: Just want you to fuck off asking to have a go of my vape.

> *A silence.*

Man looks like he's gonna cry.

> *Another silence.*

Go on then. Don't be bumming it though.

ERIC: How can you '*bum*' a vape?

DANIEL *hands* **ERIC** *the vape.*

Thank you.

ERIC *takes a long pull from the vape, then coughs up the smoke.*

He laughs through his coughs. It's infectious. **DANIEL** *can't help but join in.*

DANIEL: Child lungs. Told you.

ERIC: That's worse than doing a bong.

DANIEL *laugh loudly again.*

ERIC: What's funny?

DANIEL: What do you know about doing a bong?

ERIC: You think I was born in a shirt and tie?

DANIEL: Look like it. Give me my vape back, man.

ERIC: Or what?

DANIEL: Or I'll get my fags back out and light one of them up in here.

Beat.

ERIC: How about we go outside and you two's me on one.

DANIEL: Two's?

ERIC: Yeah.

DANIEL: Am I gonna take you to the pictures too? Maybe hold hands? Maybe get lips off you at the end of the night?

ERIC: I've quit.

DANIEL: Going to the pictures? Or giving lips?

ERIC: Just two's me on a fag will you.

DANIEL *takes out his packet of fags and throws one at* **ERIC**.

DANIEL: Have your own.

ERIC: Thank you.

DANIEL: Wanna watch them though. Give you cancer, innit.

ERIC: All gotta die of something.

He stands, gestures towards the exit.

12.

The same room.

ERIC: They are.

DANIEL: Ain't.

ERIC: Are.

DANIEL: They ain't.

ERIC: Yeah.

DANIEL: Nah.

ERIC: Trust me.

DANIEL: Bollocks.

ERIC: Why would I lie?

DANIEL: Trying to make me look a mug.

Beat.

Rah. Look at you almost getting me. Talking shit bro.

ERIC: They ain't even a north London team.

DANIEL: I must have been tripping every time I walked up the road and saw the Emirates then, innit?

ERIC: They ain't <u>proper north</u> London.

DANIEL: Says who?

ERIC: Says me. Says everyone.

DANIEL: What do you know, man?

ERIC: More than you.

DANIEL: Bollocks.

ERIC: Google it.

DANIEL: Thought this was a no phone zone?

ERIC: It is… Normally. This is the exception.

DANIEL: So we can make an exception just so you can prove your point?

ERIC: Yes.

DANIEL: That ain't fair.

ERIC: Welcome to the real world.

DANIEL: Saying I don't understand the real world now, is it?

ERIC: It's a figure of speech.

DANIEL: Saying I'm stupid?

ERIC: No, Daniel, I was just –

DANIEL: Fuck off calling me Daniel. Name's D.

ERIC: That on your birth certificate?

DANIEL: Nah, but it's on yours. Under father.

> **ERIC** *starts laughing.*

You think it's funny that I fucked your mum?

ERIC: Yes.

DANIEL: Bare funny that.

ERIC: I know. That's why I laughed.

DANIEL: I got some pictures of her on my phone. You wanna see them? That be funny as well?

ERIC: Depends what she's doing in the photos.

DANIEL: What do you reckon?

ERIC: They're your photos not mine.

DANIEL: Maybe I'll post them on Insta, yeah? Let everyone see how funny they are.

ERIC: Wouldn't mean shit to me.

DANIEL: And how's that?

ERIC: I never knew my mum. Same as you.

Pause.

DANIEL: Who said you could talk about my mum?

ERIC: I wasn't talking about your mum, I was just saying –

DANIEL: What you saying about my mum?

ERIC: I didn't –

DANIEL: You think you know me?

ERIC: I read your file.

DANIEL: Don't care what the fuck you read. You don't talk about my mum like that.

ERIC: Oh, so now mums are off limits?

DANIEL *stands pushing his chair back to the floor.*

DANIEL: WHAT THE FUCK YOU SAYING ABOUT MY FUCKING MUM, MAN?

ERIC *stands up and moves face to face with* **DANIEL**.

ERIC: I'm saying that she left. That she didn't give a fuck about you. She walked out the door. Same as mine. And people like her don't deserve kids. Don't deserve us.

Beat.

You don't leave a kid. No matter how bad it gets.

A moment.

Now pick up your chair.

DANIEL: Or what?

ERIC: Or you're gonna be standing up for the next forty minutes. And that's gonna look weird.

ERIC *returns to his seat.*

What you standing up for? Looks weird, man.

DANIEL *moves to his chair. Picks it up and rights it. Takes his seat.*

DANIEL: I alright to vape?

ERIC: Be my guest.

> **DANIEL** *takes out his vape, takes a deep lungful of smoke then blows it out.*
>
> *A heavy pause.*

ERIC: So… Woolwich. Arsenal. South London.

DANIEL: You're chatting shit man.

ERIC: Google it. I told you.

DANIEL: Vaping and phoning. Getting slack, E.

> **DANIEL** *gets his phone out and starts to tap away on it. His face falls.*
>
> That ain't right.

ERIC: Can't argue with the internet.

DANIEL: That's some fake news bullshit. The Russian's did that, innit.

ERIC: Yeah, I just wired them some Crypto before you came in.

DANIEL: You're playing me.

ERIC: Not my fault you don't know the history of your own club.

DANIEL: This ain't my club's history. This is some other team. This is –

ERIC: Say it.

DANIEL: I ain't saying it.

ERIC: You said if I could prove it, you'd say it.

DANIEL: This ain't the same thing.

ERIC: Well, if they used to be *Woolwich Arsenal*, and Woolwich is in South London, I'm pretty sure they can't be the most successful north London team, can they?

DANIEL: Fuck you man, Spurs are shit.

ERIC: And yet still the most successful North London team.

DANIEL: You ain't even a Londoner.

ERIC: South London is still London.

DANIEL: You ain't from South London.

ERIC: You want to see my driving license?

DANIEL: Point. Proved.

ERIC: What?

DANIEL: Ain't nobody born in London got a driving license. No point bruv. Tube innit.

ERIC: Maybe I have responsibilities.

DANIEL: Me too. Chore a scooter. Just as quick.

ERIC: Smart move. Then maybe you can fuck up your whole life before it's even started.

DANIEL: Don't talk to me like I'm a kid, alright? I ain't a kid.

Beat.

You gonna go tell your Fed mates that now?

ERIC: I don't have any Fed mates.

DANIEL: Psht.

ERIC: I'm a youth worker. You understand that? I'm not here to get you sent back to prison. I'm here to try and help you sort out your fucking life.

DANIEL: Just messing with you, E. No need to get all serious.

Beat.

Your accent. Can hear it when you're angry. Where is it? Manchester?

ERIC: Leeds. Yorkshire.

DANIEL: I was close.

ERIC: The two don't sound anything like –

DANIEL: Still North, innit.

ERIC: Well, yes. I suppose it is.

DANIEL: Still not London.

ERIC: You're on a roll. You fancy picking my lottery numbers while you're at it?

DANIEL: What you doing supporting Spurs then? If you're from Leeds.

A silence.

ERIC *looks away awkwardly.*

ERIC: I liked their kit when I was a kid.

DANIEL: Pah, are you a bird or something?

ERIC: Says the North Londoner supporting a South London team.

DANIEL: Shut up about that, man. Least I didn't pick my club based on their fucking kit.

ERIC: What did you base it on then?

DANIEL: Born into it innit. My old man.

ERIC: *Goonar.*

DANIEL: Don't say it like that.

ERIC: Like what?

DANIEL: Like it's a fucking disease.

Beat.

Why you move here?

ERIC: London. Streets are paved with gold.

DANIEL: Yeah. Everyone in my ends is always saying that.

ERIC: Just something you do.

DANIEL: Move away from all your family and friends?

ERIC: Ain't got no family. And anyone I knew back there definitely weren't a friend.

DANIEL: Look at you mister lone wolf.

ERIC: That's how they describe terrorists.

DANIEL: You look like a terrorist.

ERIC: Because of the colour of my skin?

DANIEL: Yeah. You got me. I'm a fucking racist. As soon as I see a black geezer wearing a suit and tie I think 'Bet that cunt's in ISIS' innit. Their usual get up.

Beat.

Coz you always look shifty, innit. Guilty. Like you've done something wrong.

ERIC: Bit prejudice that.

DANIEL: All my mates are black.

ERIC: That's what all the racists say.

DANIEL: Rah, man. I just asked you a fucking question. Just trying to find out some more about you, innit. You don't wanna answer it, then don't bother.

ERIC: I'm the one who's meant to ask you questions.

DANIEL: So you can fill in a form about me? Put me in some database. That's all this is. Box ticking. Numbers.

ERIC: You really think that?

DANIEL: What else is it?

ERIC: Maybe if you engaged you might actually find out.

DANIEL: Maybe you should get another job if you actually wanna do something more than just sign a form. How's that housing application going? You get me on a list down the council yet?

ERIC: I'm trying.

DANIEL: Yeah.

ERIC: I am, D.

A silence.

Easy place to start again.

DANIEL: What?

ERIC: Why I moved here. London. It's an easy place to start again.

DANIEL: You think?

ERIC: Worked for me.

DANIEL: Made your millions, yeah? Big city man. Tell all your crew back in Leeds how well you're doing.

ERIC: Yeah. All going to plan.

DANIEL: If I could start again it wouldn't be round here.

ERIC: Where else is there?

DANIEL: Yorkshire. Sounds nice. Sounds like fields and shit.

ERIC: You've got Finsbury Park. What you moaning about?

> **DANIEL** *laughs.*

When you're skint every where's the same. London. Leeds. Everywhere.

DANIEL: Don't look like you're going skint any time soon, mister suit and tie man.

ERIC: T K Max. It'll change your life.

DANIEL: Not my style.

ERIC: Can't see your *roadman* style helping for interviews.

DANIEL: Depends on the interview.

ERIC: Promising career you have there in GBH and intent to supply.

DANIEL: I didn't *GBH* no one.

ERIC: Not what it says on your record.

DANIEL: Feds stitched me up.

ERIC: Bit of a cliché that.

DANIEL: Joint enterprise. Weren't me who hit the lad.

ERIC: You just watched?

DANIEL: You think me stepping in would have helped? You reckon I wouldn't just end up getting a pasting like him?

ERIC: He lost an eye.

DANIEL: He was a grass.

ERIC: He lost. An eye.

DANIEL: Shouldn't have been grassing then should he. Maybe then it wouldn't have happened.

ERIC: Bad for business. Grasses. In your line of work.

DANIEL: Got to earn, innit.

ERIC: Shit pension plan though. Dealing.

DANIEL: Pensions are fucked man. You not watch the news?

ERIC: So you're gonna be a millionaire shotting some weed round the estate, yeah?

DANIEL: Maybe.

ERIC: Can't move for millionaire hoodrats. What everyone's saying.

DANIEL: You don't see.

ERIC: I see perfectly. Unlike that poor lad you and your mates –

DANIEL: I DIDN'T DO FUCK ALL TO THAT KID.

Pause.

ERIC: You were shotting on the estate.

DANIEL: Everyone's shotting on the estate.

ERIC: Makes it alright then?

DANIEL: Job, innit. How much you bank doing this shit?

ERIC: How much time you done in Feltham?

Beat.

DANIEL: I ain't saying I don't feel bad about what happened to the boy. His eye. But it weren't by my hand. I've done my time. Said my sorrys. Just trying to move on, innit.

ERIC: Move on to what?

DANIEL: This. Life.

Beat.

Maybe you get me out from here and I can do that.

ERIC: I'm trying.

DANIEL: Try harder.

A silence.

You gonna ask me these questions for your form then, mister suit and tie, tick box man, or what?

ERIC: You gonna answer them?

DANIEL: Might do. Can't have you losing your big man job and both of us ending up on the rock and roll, can we?

13.

The same room.

Lots of paper lies scattered across the floor.

DANIEL: Why everyone always just assume shit like that?

ERIC: I didn't.

DANIEL: It's a cuss, man.

ERIC: How is it a cuss?

DANIEL: *Music and Sport.* For fucksake.

ERIC: You like music. You like sport. You told me that.

DANIEL: Yeah but it don't mean that's all I was any good at at school, does it? That's like the classes that the fucking dumb cunts get their GCSE from, innit. *Can't read and write, no worries, sing a couple of bars, go run over there as quick as you can.* Sweet, two GCSEs, go tell mummy and daddy and they'll buy you a fucking car.

ERIC: What did you get your GCSEs in then?

DANIEL: Don't fucking matter. Just coz I've got a GCSE in science don't mean they're gonna give me a lab coat and call me a fucking chemist, does it?

ERIC: I was just trying to work out what you're interested in.

DANIEL: What I'm interested in ain't gonna make me any money is it?

ERIC: You don't know that.

DANIEL: If that was how easy life is, why you think there are people who become traffic wardens?

ERIC: Maybe that is what they're interested in.

DANIEL: Getting called a cunt all day, everyday, by everyone?

ERIC: Helping the community.

A moment.

ERIC *can't hold it anymore, he bursts out laughing.* **DANIEL** *sees he was taking the piss and joins in.*

DANIEL: Traffic wardens, man.

ERIC: Fucking hate traffic wardens.

DANIEL: Do look like they enjoy themselves though, innit? Maybe they've got it sussed. Out in the sun all day. Probably blazing. Sounds sweet.

ERIC: Out in the sun?

DANIEL: Yeah.

ERIC: Where do you live? It's sunny here for about a week a year.

DANIEL: Better than in some fucking shop selling trainers.

ERIC: Yeah, that's the only other job isn't it.

DANIEL: Can't all be a fucking headshrinker.

ERIC: Headshrinker?

DANIEL: Yeah fam. You. Trying to fix my head, innit. PhD in chat.

ERIC: I ain't got a PhD in nothing.

DANIEL: Then I demand I get a qualified one of you lot. You're fired.

ERIC: Fuck it, I quit.

A shared moment.

What do you want to do?

DANIEL: Maybe go get a beer and watch the football, you game?

ERIC: You know what I mean.

DANIEL: Why do we have to do these sessions on Champions League nights?

ERIC: Not like it affects you anymore.

DANIEL: You can talk. And anyway, fuck you man. Arsenal will be back. They're just in transition.

Pause.

ERIC: You just gonna avoid the question?

DANIEL: It don't matter.

ERIC: Course it does.

DANIEL: People like me don't get to choose what we do. Ain't like that round here.

ERIC: You can still have a dream. Aspirations.

DANIEL: Fuck me man, we gonna blow out a candle and make a wish as well?

ERIC: If you want.

DANIEL: No cake. And it ain't no one's birthday.

A silence. **ERIC** *looks awkward.* **DANIEL** *notices this.*

It ain't, is it?

ERIC: Not a big deal when you get to my age.

DANIEL: Fuck man, what you doing here on your birthday?

ERIC: It's only for a couple of hours.

DANIEL: Even so.

ERIC: This is important.

DANIEL: Not as important as your birthday, fam!

ERIC: You're my last appointment.

DANIEL: There's others? You're cheating on me with other delinquents? I'm hurt, E.

ERIC: Man's gotta eat.

DANIEL: You like me the best though, innit?

ERIC: I like all of you.

Pause.

DANIEL: Shit, bro, you're blushing. Do you love me?

DANIEL *stands and opens his arms towards* **ERIC**.

Come here and get some birthday love, man.

ERIC: Maybe we could get back to the session then I'll be home in time
for –

DANIEL: Give me the form. I'll mark you in and you can slip out. Go get
yourself some birthday fun.

ERIC: I'll have some fun when I get home.

DANIEL: Oh yeah?

ERIC: Yeah.

DANIEL: Mrs Eric gonna put on a show, eh?

ERIC: Watch your mouth.

Beat.

DANIEL: A chef.

ERIC: What?

DANIEL: I wanted to be a chef.

ERIC: Yeah?

DANIEL: Can't have everyone eating Maccie Dees for the rest of their
lives, innit. All end up with a body like yours.

ERIC: Funny.

DANIEL: Weren't joking.

ERIC: Long hours, cheffing.

DANIEL: Saying I'm scared of a bit of graft?

ERIC: Don't get paid a lot either.

DANIEL: Yeah, Jamie Oliver's proper skint ain't he? Saw the cunt asking for a quid outside Holloway tube last week.

Pause.

ERIC: I've got a few mates who work in the food industry.

DANIEL: Told you, I'm not interested in working at Maccie Dees.

ERIC: I'm serious.

DANIEL: So am I.

Beat.

What kind of places they work in?

14.

The same room.

DANIEL *stands on a chair looking out of a window. The sound of a siren can be heard in the background. Moments pass.*

ERIC *enters. Stops. Looks at* **DANIEL**.

DANIEL: What the pigs doing?

ERIC: The *police* are taking him in.

DANIEL: Weren't even doing nothing.

ERIC: Shotting weed is nothing?

DANIEL: Ain't exactly Pablo Escobar, is he?

ERIC: Everyone starts somewhere.

DANIEL: Why they ramming his arm up his back like that?

ERIC: They're arresting him.

DANIEL: Yeah but it's pretty hard to resist arrest when you've got two people sitting on your back.

ERIC: Come down.

DANIEL: They're gonna break his arm.

ERIC: No more scooter joyriding for him.

DANIEL: Why you being all chill about this?

ERIC: I spoke to the police. They told me what was going on. I came back inside.

DANIEL: Not your problem, nah?

ERIC: No.

DANIEL: Just look the other way then, yeah?

ERIC: He got caught trying to sell some weed to a thirteen year old.

DANIEL: You never smoked a bit of weed?

ERIC: I've never sold it.

DANIEL: You think it just grows on trees?

Beat.

ERIC: You do know how stupid that sounded?

DANIEL: Fuck you.

DANIEL *shouts towards the window.*

Oi! What the fuck do you think you're doing!

ERIC: Will you shut up for fucksake.

DANIEL: You seen what they're doing to him?

ERIC: And you think you shouting is gonna help?

DANIEL *turns around to face* **ERIC**.

DANIEL: Better than you standing there and doing fuck all.

ERIC: D…

DANIEL: What?

ERIC: There's still other kids here. Youth workers.

DANIEL: And?

ERIC: I just don't want this to turn into a / situ –

DANIEL: Oi! Get the fuck off him, Fed!

ERIC: Daniel!

DANIEL *steps down from the chair.*

Right let's get back –

DANIEL: Fuck that.

DANIEL *moves towards the door.* **ERIC** *blocks his path.*

Get out of my way, man.

ERIC: You wanna go back inside?

DANIEL: How's that?

ERIC: Breaking the terms of your license.

DANIEL: For what? Telling a Fed not to snap a guy's arm?

ERIC: If you go out there it's going to kick off. You know that.

DANIEL: Well maybe shit needs to kick off.

ERIC: Just leave it.

DANIEL: You leave it.

ERIC *shoves* **DANIEL** *backwards.*

A moment of stillness. Both men shocked at this.

DANIEL: Like that is it?

ERIC: I'm sorry, I didn't –

DANIEL *walks past him and off towards the door.*

You just don't get it do you. You haven't got the first fucking idea. It's so easy for you.

DANIEL: Easy?

ERIC: Yeah.

DANIEL: How's that then?

Pause.

Coz I'm white? That it?

ERIC: I didn't say that.

DANIEL: Meant it though.

ERIC: You fucking child.

DANIEL: Say that again. I dare you.

ERIC: Big man.

DANIEL: Big enough to go out there and help a man. Don't see you rushing out there.

ERIC: Because I know what will happen.

DANIEL: You worried he's gonna get popped? No. That *you're* gonna get popped? That's it isn't it? Fed ain't got guns over here, E. So calm yourself.

ERIC: You have no idea what it's like to be stopped by the police when you're a –

DANIEL: We're all same to them, E. All of us round here. Poor. Black. Same fucking thing.

A moment.

You think I'm wrong?

ERIC: I think you don't know the first fucking thing about your privilege –

DANIEL: My privilege? You taking the fucking piss? I grew up on the estate where more people get merked than go university. I had a crackhead for a father and a mother who fucked off before I'd said my first word. Ain't ever got shit I ain't worked for. Ain't had nothing. Second hand fucking hoody and a happy meal for dinner if I can scrape together four fucking quid. *My privilege.* Fuck. That's some university posh person shit. Round here that don't play.

ERIC: You really don't know what the fuck you're talking about, do you?

DANIEL: Know enough.

ERIC: The difference is they don't need a fucking excuse to fuck with me. I don't have to be doing some silly shit on an estate.

DANIEL: You not doing some silly shit ever then, nah?

ERIC: Fuck you.

DANIEL: Swearing is he? Wanna watch that bruv. Get you in trouble.

ERIC: Was he coming here to meet you?

A silence.

Was he dropping off the weed here to you?

DANIEL: You think I'm dumb?

ERIC: Just answer the question.

DANIEL: I've only been out ten weeks.

ERIC: And?

DANIEL: You think I wanna get sent back for a little bit of smoke?

ERIC: You tell me.

Pause.

DANIEL *turns and walks back to his chair. Sits.*

DANIEL: Man shouldn't have been shotting to thirteen year olds.

ERIC: No.

DANIEL: Bad choices.

ERIC: Yes.

DANIEL: I didn't ring him.

ERIC: No?

DANIEL: First time I've seen him since Feltham. Just chatting shit, innit. Catching up.

ERIC: You buy any off him?

DANIEL: He gave me a teenth.

ERIC: For fucksake.

DANIEL: I asked you to get me out of here. What you fucking think's gonna happen? I do a bit of time and come out and the whole fucking world's gone straight? This place, man. It's a memory. A fucking memory with hands grabbing at me. Pulling me back down.

Pause.

ERIC: Give it to me.

DANIEL: It's a fucking ten bag man, come on.

ERIC: Say the police come in here and want us to give statements?

DANIEL: Don't think they've got the sniffer dogs with them, fam.

ERIC: You want to take that chance?

Beat.

Thought you wanted me to try and get you that work experience at my mate's restaurant?

DANIEL *rummages in his pocket and pulls out the weed. Throws it to* **ERIC**.

DANIEL: Don't be getting high on mine's though.

ERIC: That's it?

A moment.

DANIEL: Thank you.

ERIC: You're welcome.

Beat.

You got any rizla?

He smiles.

15.

The same room.

ERIC *is sat in a chair waiting. He looks absolutely knackered.*

We see his head nod. He's virtually asleep.

DANIEL *enters. Sees* **ERIC**.

DANIEL: Wakey, wakey, bro!

Beat.

ERIC: You're late.

DANIEL: You're snoozing.

ERIC: I wasn't.

DANIEL: Proper bags under your eyes. Wanna watch that bro. Gotta get your beauty sleep.

ERIC *takes out a vape and takes a long blast from it.*

Rah, look at you on the vape, E. I've converted you.

ERIC: You haven't converted shit.

DANIEL: Look at you. Pluming, bro. What's the voltage on that bad boy?

ERIC: That isn't important.

DANIEL: Course it is fam, you ratchet that bad boy up too high and you'll be fucked quicker than a Spurs fan in the Emirate's toilet.

ERIC: This isn't funny.

DANIEL: You're telling me, man. Burning through coils is no laughing matter.

He sniffs at the air. Smiles.

That's paradise too, innit? You've even yoinked my flavour.

ERIC: The trial shift? At the restaurant?

Pause.

DANIEL: Ah, yeah man, I meant to ring you –

ERIC: But you didn't.

DANIEL: You my mum now, bro?

ERIC: No. Coz I actually give a fuck about you.

Beat.

I sorted that. Wasn't some fucking government bullshit. No back to work scheme. I did that. I asked a favour from a mate for you. I vouched for you.

DANIEL: Weren't me who kept going on about it.

ERIC: You were the one who –

DANIEL: Just going along with you, innit.

ERIC: No, you weren't, I saw how –

DANIEL: More than happy as I am.

ERIC: Yeah, course you are.

DANIEL: Look at me smiling.

He smiles.

ERIC: Are you high?

DANIEL: On life.

ERIC: This isn't fucking funny, D.

DANIEL: Why you stressing man?

ERIC: You made me look a dick.

DANIEL: Ain't me who gave you your looks.

ERIC: Fuck this.

DANIEL: I'm a busy man, E. Didn't know this was so important to you.

ERIC: It wasn't important to me. It was important to you.

DANIEL: Dunno why you're making such a big deal out of it.

ERIC *picks up his bag.*

What you doing?

ERIC: I'm going.

DANIEL: Going where?

ERIC: Anywhere.

DANIEL: E…

ERIC *is now walking to the exit.*

Eric, man. Please.

ERIC: Please what? Please let tell you a load of shit about how I wanna be a chef, then when I sort you out a chance to get some experience you just don't turn up? Is that it? Well fuck that. I've got better things to be doing with my time.

ERIC *is at the door.*

DANIEL: I bottled it. Alright? I fucking shit it.

Beat.

What they gonna think, me turning up at some posh restaurant in my fucking jeans looking like a cunt.

ERIC: They wanted to give you a chance.

DANIEL: I don't want a fucking chance. I just… I just…

ERIC: What?

DANIEL: I wanna be normal, yeah? I wanna be a normal person. Just go about my business and that. Do my thing.

ERIC: And you could have. You just had to turn up.

DANIEL: And them all look at me and think 'crim', yeah? *Look at this cunt, not even eighteen and got a sheet. Look at his clothes. Don't fit.* Ain't ever gonna fit.

ERIC: I didn't tell them how I knew you.

DANIEL: You ever filled in a job application? Full disclosure bro. Ain't no hiding that shit.

ERIC: It was just a trial shift.

DANIEL: Yeah and then what if it went well? What if they ask me to stay?

ERIC: They might have understood.

DANIEL: Yeah. In fucking cloud cuckoo land.

ERIC: So, this is it then? Just do fuck all?

DANIEL: And what if it is?

ERIC: Well that's a great plan. That way you can never get rejected. You can never fail at anything. And now you've got an excuse to never try and actually do anything for the whole of your fucking life. Well fucking done.

ERIC starts clapping. DANIEL mockingly joins in.

DANIEL: You don't understand shit.

ERIC: Nah. Course not. I'm the idiot. Me and everyone else.

DANIEL: What's that meant to mean?

ERIC: Oh fuck, the big man doesn't understand something, there's a fucking sur –

DANIEL: You wanna stop talking at me like that.

ERIC: Why? Coz you know so much? Coz you're so wise.

DANIEL: Wise enough to know I ain't getting no job at no fancy restaurant. Wise enough to know shit like that don't happen to people like me.

ERIC: Us. People like us.

Beat.

DANIEL: Yeah?

ERIC: Yeah.

Pause.

DANIEL: Bad man is he? What'd you do, mister badman?

ERIC: I don't want to talk about it.

DANIEL: What'd you do?

ERIC: It's not important.

DANIEL: Yeah it is. You come here asking me all these questions every week and I can't ask you one back? What's that?

ERIC: I said I don't want to talk about it.

DANIEL: You mug an old lady? Nah, looks more like one of them accountants that rips off his client, innit.

ERIC: Daniel.

DANIEL: Pussy crime. White collar bullshit.

Beat.

Hold up, you didn't touch up any kids did you –

ERIC: YOU THINK THAT'S FUCKING FUNNY FUCKING CARRY ON YEAH KEEP PUSHING SEE WHAT HAPPENS.

DANIEL: E –

ERIC: Few months in kiddy prison and thinks he can come here and talk to me. You know what happens if you go big boy prison? You know what that's like, you smart fucking cunt?

A silence.

DANIEL: I'm sorry, E. Just banter innit.

ERIC: Nah it fucking ain't.

DANIEL: E…

ERIC: Why do you think I do this?

DANIEL: PhD in chat innit.

ERIC: Stop it. Stop taking the piss. Just for one minute.

DANIEL: I don't fucking know do I.

Pause.

You gonna fuck me off now?

ERIC: What?

DANIEL: Like Brian? Wash you hands, izzit?

ERIC: No. Of course I'm not.

DANIEL: Nah?

ERIC: This is important to me. You're –

DANIEL: Mister suit and tie man. Mister turned it all around and wants to give back man.

ERIC: And what's so wrong with that?

DANIEL: Coz it ain't always the same. Ain't everyone get out.

ERIC: Get out from what?

DANIEL: The shit. Everyday it's still here. Same fucking schemes. Same people saying *Why you trying to turn straight? What's the point?* How many fucking times I ask you? Get me a new crib. Then maybe I can turn up at your fancy restaurant. It's you. All of you. All your big talk and *We can all change if we want* bullshit. How about you just do what I fucking ask you, hey?

ERIC: I tried. Okay. I fucking tried.

DANIEL: Yeah so you keep on saying.

ERIC: You know how many phone calls I made trying to get you on that list?

DANIEL: So it's alright for you to just give up but when I –

ERIC: I didn't give up. It's not the same thing.

DANIEL: Sounds the same to me.

ERIC: Fuck you.

DANIEL: Nah man, fuck you. You're a liar.

ERIC: What makes you so special, eh? What means you should jump to the top of the housing list? There's people out there who actually try. People who are actually turning up and giving it a fucking go and they can't get anywhere near it. But you? Nah, you just expect it don't you?

Pause.

DANIEL: Bank more in a weekend on the estate than I would in that kitchen anyway.

ERIC: Yeah. You probably would.

DANIEL: What's the point then?

ERIC: I don't know. I honestly don't know.

DANIEL: Fuck about trying to fit in. Trying to graft.

ERIC: Yeah.

Pause.

DANIEL: You reverse psycologising me again bro?

ERIC: I'm just tired.

DANIEL: Yeah me too. From the moment I fucking wake up.

A moment. **ERIC** *takes out a pen. Signs the form.*

ERIC: Here's your form.

DANIEL: We've still got time left.

ERIC: It's fine. I've signed you off. Go and do whatever.

Beat.

DANIEL: E…

ERIC: No, it's fine. It's not a thing.

DANIEL: It is man. I can tell. I know –

ERIC: We'll start again next week. See if we can find something else.

DANIEL: I don't –

ERIC: It's fine.

> **DANIEL** *passes* **ERIC** *a piece of paper.* **ERIC** *signs it.* **DANIEL** *lingers.*

> I'll see you next week. We're good. Promise.

DANIEL: Peace, yeah.

ERIC: Peace.

> **DANIEL** *exits.*

> **ERIC** *lets his head fall into his hands.*

16.

The street. Night.

DANIEL *stands alone. A rucksack on his back.*

He paces. Takes out a cigarette, lights it.

ERIC *enters.*

DANIEL: What took you so long?

ERIC: It's the middle of the night.

DANIEL: It's ten o'clock.

ERIC: That is the middle of the night when you've got kids.

> *Beat.*

> Why did you ring me?

DANIEL: You said I could ring you. You gave me your number.

ERIC: For the trial shift at my mate's restaurant. Not just so you can call me any –

DANIEL: Why you making me feel bad about ringing you man?

ERIC: I'm not.

He softens.

I'm not.

DANIEL: I shouldn't have come.

ERIC: Is this about the last session?

DANIEL *looks away from* **ERIC**. *Starts to pace again.*

DANIEL: I didn't want to involve you in this. I promise. I just…

ERIC: What's happened?

DANIEL: I didn't have no one else I could call. No one I could talk to. Not without it getting back to them.

ERIC: You can talk to me.

Pause.

D. Come on. Whatever it is we can sort it out.

DANIEL *takes his bag off and opens it, revealing its contents.*

Where the fuck did you get that?

DANIEL: It ain't mine.

ERIC: Then where the fuck did you get it?

DANIEL: Just someone.

ERIC: *Just someone.*

DANIEL: Yeah.

ERIC: Is it real?

DANIEL: Looks real.

ERIC: And what are you going to do with it?

Beat.

DANIEL: Look at me like that.

ERIC: What?

DANIEL: I see it. All over your face.

ERIC: What the fuck do you want me to say? You call me up in the middle of the night –

DANIEL: It ain't mine. I ain't gonna use it.

ERIC: Then what the fuck are you doing with it?

DANIEL: They told me to take it. What else am I gonna do, eh?

ERIC: Say 'no'.

DANIEL: You think these are the kind of people you say 'no' to?

> **ERIC** *takes out his phone.*

What you doing?

ERIC: I'm going to call the police.

> **DANIEL** *grabs* **ERIC***'s phone from him.*

DANIEL: Fuck off, man.

ERIC: Give me my phone back.

DANIEL: So you can call the Feds?

ERIC: You know this breaks the terms of your license.

DANIEL: No shit.

ERIC: I have a duty to report this.

DANIEL: Yeah?

> *Pause.*

Do it then. Send me to *big boy* prison. Maybe you can help them put me back in cuffs too. Push me in the back of the meat wagon so they can take me back to nick.

> **DANIEL** *passes him back the phone.*

Go on, do it.

> *A moment.*

ERIC: You've fucked us now. Both of us. You know that?

ERIC *puts his phone back in his pocket.*

Who gave you it?

DANIEL: I'm not a grass.

ERIC: I can't help you if you don't tell me.

DANIEL: What does it matter?

ERIC: Because we could go to the police and –

DANIEL: Thought you said you understood. *People like us*, yeah? That's what you said.

ERIC: I'm trying to help.

DANIEL: By getting me killed?

ERIC: What did they tell you to do with it?

DANIEL: Lose it.

ERIC: This just keeps getting better.

DANIEL: It ain't like they've popped someone with it.

ERIC: How do you know that? How the fuck do you know that?

DANIEL: I googled it.

Pause.

ERIC: What?

DANIEL: You know. Whether anything had happened lately. Robberies, you know. Merks.

ERIC: Googled?

DANIEL: Yeah.

ERIC: Well, everything's peachy fucking creamy then, isn't it?

DANIEL: I DIDN'T KNOW WHAT TO DO, OKAY? THAT'S WHY I FUCKING CALLED YOU.

Beat.

I'm scared, E. I didn't want this. None of this. I'm trying man. I'm fucking trying.

Pause.

Might as well just fucking use it on myself, innit. Only fucking way out of here.

A silence.

ERIC: Give it to me.

DANIEL: You gonna go and hand it in?

ERIC: I'm going to *lose* it.

DANIEL: You promise?

ERIC: I said it, didn't I?

> **DANIEL** *reaches inside his bag.*

The bag. Give me the bag. I'm not going to walk around with a piece tucked in my belt like a fucking gangster.

He does.

Go home. Forget about it. It's sorted, okay.

DANIEL: I can come with you?

ERIC: I'll see you at the session next week. Just like normal.

> **ERIC** *swings the bag round on to his back and starts towards the exit.*

DANIEL: E…

He stops and turns back.

I didn't have anyone else to call.

Beat.

I'm sorry.

17

The room.

DANIEL *sits alone.*

Moments pass.

DANIEL *takes out his vape. Smokes.*

He takes out his phone. Dials a number.

DANIEL: E, where you at fam. Two minutes and I'm lighting up a blunt in here.

He hangs up the phone and puts it away.

He takes out a cigarette. Lights it.

Starts to smoke.

18.

The same room.

DANIEL *enters, sees the room is empty.*

He plays with his phone.

Moments pass.

He gets out a chair and sits down.

19.

The office.

SARA *and* **ERIC** *sit.*

SARA: So you're feeling better?

ERIC: Yeah.

SARA: A cold, was it?

ERIC: Flu.

SARA: A lot of it going about at the minute.

ERIC: I'm glad to be back.

SARA: And your wife?

ERIC: Yeah she's sick of me being at home too.

SARA: I meant is she okay.

ERIC: She is.

SARA: Didn't catch it off you?

ERIC: No.

SARA: And the baby?

ERIC: No.

SARA: So everything's okay?

ERIC: Yes.

SARA: You're sure.

ERIC: I just said so, didn't I?

SARA: Good. Because if there is an issue…

ERIC: There's not.

Pause.

SARA: I wasn't always the boss, Eric. I did ten years on the front lines.

ERIC: I know.

SARA: If you wanted to talk to me…

ERIC: We're talking now.

SARA: You know what I mean.

ERIC: I'm fine.

Pause.

SARA: I looked into that housing request for Daniel.

ERIC: Really? I thought you said –

SARA: It's a no, sadly.

ERIC: Oh. Right.

SARA: Just the way it is.

ERIC: Yeah.

20.

The room.

ERIC *sits alone.*

Moments pass.

DANIEL *enters the room. He stops.*

A silence.

DANIEL: Back izzit?

ERIC: Yeah.

DANIEL: Bout time.

ERIC: Daniel…

DANIEL: Was telling one of the boys you'd probably shit it as the North London derby was coming up.

ERIC: I'm confident.

DANIEL: You lot always say that. Then you lose.

>   *Beat.*

>   You got my bag?

>   *A silence.*

>   Knew you'd chored it and done the off. If you couldn't afford one, would have just given it to you.

ERIC: Don't.

DANIEL: What?

ERIC: Make a joke out of what happened.

DANIEL: I look like I'm joking?

ERIC: Feels like you are.

DANIEL: You wanna talk it through then? Wanna make sure that we're both okay? That there ain't been no blow back or shit that's come of it?

ERIC: I'm trying to talk to you –

DANIEL: A little bit fucking late if you ask me.

Pause.

ERIC: I don't think you get to speak to me like that. Not now.

DANIEL: I ain't the one who went fucking awol, bruv.

A silence.

ERIC: I wanted to call you.

DANIEL: Funny, coz my phone's been on. Maybe I should ring O2, everyone always says their service is shit.

ERIC: I wanted to.

DANIEL: Didn't though, did you? Left me hanging here like some mug.

ERIC: They said they would get someone to do the sessions while I was away.

DANIEL: Yeah coz that's the important thing, innit.

ERIC: These sessions are important.

DANIEL: Why'd you give me the fuck me off and let some prick cover you like it's nothing then?

Pause.

ERIC: What was the other guy like?

DANIEL: Some posh old dude.

ERIC: Yeah?

DANIEL: Tourists. The lot of you.

Pause.

ERIC: He like football?

DANIEL: Supported Fulham.

ERIC: Fulham?

DANIEL: He was from Hackney.

ERIC: He get lost on the way to Harrods?

DANIEL: You really one to talk about that?

Beat.

Knew his box sets though. Gotta give him that. Linked me up with loads of shit to watch and that. Even leant me some DVDs.

ERIC: DVDs?

DANIEL: Yeah, the old prick. Man's house must be like a museum.

ERIC *smiles.*

ERIC: How much did you get for them?

DANIEL *laughs.*

DANIEL: Couple of quid. Hard fucking sell though, bro. Had to visit some old people's home to find anyone interested.

ERIC: I've still got a DVD player.

DANIEL: You proving my point for me, E.

ERIC *smiles.*

DANIEL: Cunt won't miss them. Might get off his arse and get a proper job now, innit.

ERIC: That's really good of you to help him

DANIEL: Maybe if you'd have rocked up then he wouldn't be having gaps in his collection.

ERIC: I'm not the one who fucked this up! I'm not the one who…

Pause, he regains his composure.

DANIEL: The one who what?

Beat.

The one. Who. What?

Silence.

ERIC: I've got a kid. A wife. I can't fuck that up.

DANIEL: I didn't ask you to.

ERIC: I need to set boundaries.

DANIEL: I ain't gonna try and touch your tits.

ERIC: I'm not joking.

DANIEL: Neither am I.

ERIC: I shouldn't have given you my mobile number.

DANIEL: I thought we were mates, yeah?

ERIC: I'm your youth worker.

DANIEL: Cold.

ERIC: I like you.

DANIEL: Why does it feel like you're giving me the flick then?

ERIC: I'm not.

DANIEL: Feels like you are.

ERIC: I just think we need to focus more –

DANIEL: Focus on what?

ERIC: Setting some long-term goals. Trying to find you a job. Concentrating more on what these sessions are meant to be –

DANIEL: Why you being like this?

ERIC: So me trying to help you get a job isn't a good thing?

DANIEL: You ring your mate in the restaurant again?

Pause.

Nah, thought not.

Beat.

Look at you looking away.

ERIC: I'm not.

DANIEL: Yeah you are. Ashamed now, izzit? No good to you anymore?

Beat.

ERIC: I've brought in some more job specs I thought we could go through them together…

DANIEL *stands up with his bag and starts to walk towards the door.*

The session's not over yet.

DANIEL: Yeah it is.

ERIC: If you leave I'll have to mark it down as an incomplete session.

DANIEL: Do what the fuck you want.

ERIC: Daniel…

DANIEL *exits.*

D!

21.

The office.

SARA: Communication?

A silence.

ERIC: One

SARA: Working with others?

ERIC: One.

SARA: Setting and achieving goals?

ERIC: One.

SARA: Confidence?

ERIC: Four.

SARA: Reliability?

ERIC: Four.

SARA: Leadership skills?

ERIC: One.

SARA: Managing feelings?

A beat…

22.

The community centre.

DANIEL *sits opposite* **ERIC** *vaping continuously.*

A long silence.

ERIC: Seriously, you are shit at staring competitions.

Another silence.

We've only got a couple of sessions left. You could at least humour me for them.

DANIEL: Wouldn't want to break any of your boundaries.

ERIC: That's not fair.

DANIEL: Your words not mine.

ERIC: Don't be a dick.

DANIEL: If you ain't got nothing nice to say then maybe don't say nothing at all, bruv.

ERIC: Very clever.

Beat.

You wanna tell me what you've been up to?

DANIEL: No.

ERIC: Have you looked at any of the vacancies I emailed you?

DANIEL: I'm bored man. This is long.

ERIC: Don't do that.

DANIEL: Just telling you the truth, innit.

ERIC: No you're not.

DANIEL: Knows me, does he?

ERIC: We've already established that.

DANIEL: Same as me, is he?

ERIC: I didn't say that.

DANIEL: Gonna tell your *mum* story. Tell your *I've done time* story. What you trying to prove? You a big man? You someone back in the day? Ain't shit now. Look at you. You no one.

ERIC: I was someone when you needed my help.

DANIEL: Then what? Then you disappear.

ERIC: I apologised.

DANIEL: Too late.

ERIC: It's never too late.

    DANIEL *starts pissing himself laughing.*

DANIEL: You been reading your youth worker books again, E?

ERIC: Don't take the piss.

DANIEL: Don't say stupid shit out of a fairy story then.

ERIC: So this is it then? This is how it's going to be now?

DANIEL: I'm here, ain't I?

ERIC: Not really.

DANIEL: Looks like I'm here.

ERIC: We were making progress. We were getting somewhere. Don't just throw all that away.

DANIEL: How the fuck you think this ends? You gonna save me, E? That it? Gonna get me back on the straight and narrow. Go tell your new posh London friends how you did some good?

ERIC: No, I –

DANIEL: How you gave something back? How you turned your life round and now look at you. Mister fucking shining example.

ERIC: This isn't about me.

DANIEL: What is it about then?

ERIC: Us. Both of us.

DANIEL: We mates? That it? We gonna hang out when this is all done?

Pause.

Nah, course not. You got a family ain't you. Real family.

ERIC: What do you want me to do?

DANIEL: Admit it. It's bollocks. All of this.

ERIC: No.

DANIEL: So I bump into you on the street in the real world, you gonna slap me on the back? Ask me if I fancy going and having a couple of pints? Watch the game? Take me home to meet your wife? Your son? Maybe if I have a kid then they can play together. That it?

ERIC: I'd like that.

DANIEL: Then why the fuck didn't you call me?

A silence.

ERIC: I fucked up.

DANIEL: Yeah you did.

ERIC: I know this might come as some cosmic surprise, but the whole fucking world doesn't revolve around you. You think I want to handle a piece? Go back and look at my son after doing that? Get in bed with my wife? You think I want to jeopardise everything I've worked for? Every single part of my life that I somehow managed to put back together again since I got here?

DANIEL: Long as you're alright –

ERIC: Stop it. Just stop doing that.

DANIEL: I didn't want none of this. Wanted to change. Sort myself out. But it ain't like that is it? Ain't no changing for people like me.

ERIC: So you're just gonna give up?

DANIEL: What's my other options?

ERIC: Give me another chance.

Pause.

DANIEL: I ain't worth all this aggro, E.

ERIC: I think you are.

DANIEL: You don't know me.

A silence.

ERIC: So what then, we just sit here and stare at each other?

DANIEL: You might finally win one of these competitions, we do it long enough.

ERIC *laughs.*

ERIC: That's some proper Arsenal humour there.

DANIEL: We're in transition, bruv.

ERIC: You're always in transition.

DANIEL: Ain't that the truth.

ERIC: Least we ain't Fulham fans.

Beat.

You got any of his DVDs left?

DANIEL: Might have.

ERIC: Anything good?

DANIEL: Yeah a few. You wanna see the list?

ERIC: How many did he give you?!

DANIEL: Got more titles than Netflix, bro.

Beat.

ERIC: Show me the list.

DANIEL: You thinking you'll be getting a discount?

ERIC: Mate's rates?

DANIEL: Think we're pals again, izzit?

Pause.

Fuck it. Mate's rates.

23.

The office.

SARA: Setting and achieving goals?

ERIC: Three.

SARA: Confidence?

ERIC: Three.

SARA: Reliability?

ERIC: Three.

   Pause.

SARA: Leadership skills?

ERIC: Three.

SARA: Managing feelings?

   A beat…

24.

The community centre.

DANIEL *sits holding his face.* **ERIC** *stands near him fussing.*

DANIEL: I'm fine.

ERIC: Just let me see.

DANIEL: I'm fine, E. Just leave me alone.

ERIC: There's blood on your clothes.

   There is.

   Let me see, Daniel.

   ERIC *puts a hand on* **DANIEL**'s, **DANIEL** *winces back in pain.*

DANIEL: Fuck, man!

ERIC: Sorry.

   He moves back from **DANIEL**.

Please. I just want to make sure you're –

DANIEL moves his hands down from his face. His eyes are bruised and on one side of his face his mouth has been slit upwards in a Chelsea smile type fashion; it's been stitched up, but the cut is so fresh it's still weeping.

DANIEL: Okay?

ERIC: We need to get you to a hospital.

DANIEL: Already been, fam. You think my old man stitched me up?

ERIC: It's still bleeding.

DANIEL: Yeah, that's what happens when someone slashes your face.

ERIC: Fuck.

DANIEL: Not wanna take me to the pictures and give me lips no more, E?

ERIC: Don't make jokes about this.

DANIEL: It's my fucking face! It's my fucking face they slit up! So I'll make jokes about whatever I fucking want.

Pause.

ERIC: Who did that to you?

DANIEL: Some prick.

ERIC: Was it to do with…

Beat.

DANIEL: Ark at you worrying about yourself.

ERIC: Was it?

DANIEL: Nah, fam. So calm yourself.

A moment.

ERIC: I'm sorry.

DANIEL: Don't be. You got kin, innit. Need to know they're safe.

ERIC: Are you safe?

DANIEL: Reckon if they'd wanted to do me, then I'd be done.

ERIC: You look pretty done.

DANIEL: Talk about kick a man when he's down.

ERIC: Who did it?

DANIEL: Just a scuffle that went wrong.

ERIC: So wrong they slashed your face?

DANIEL: Getting spicy out there now. Everyone got something to prove.

ERIC: They always did.

DANIEL: Not like now. I'm lucky, innit. Better a slash than acid in the mush.

ERIC: *Lucky*.

DANIEL: Yeah.

   Pause.

ERIC: You back selling?

DANIEL: You buying?

ERIC: D…

DANIEL: Just bits. Nothing serious.

ERIC: I have to report this.

DANIEL: Yeah, that's gonna help, innit.

ERIC: What if they come back?

DANIEL: Ain't no come back. Already told you.

ERIC: You don't know that.

DANIEL: I know I don't wanna talk about it.

ERIC: I can't sit here and act normal when your face looks like that.

DANIEL: I been thinking the same about you since the first session.

   A silence.

ERIC: Let me make the call.

DANIEL: Ain't no good comes of that.

ERIC: I'd know you're safe.

DANIEL: Nah, you wouldn't.

Beat.

I had a look at some of those jobs you sent me.

ERIC: Yeah?

DANIEL: Yeah.

ERIC: Any that take your fancy?

DANIEL: The JD Sports one.

ERIC: Thought you'd like that.

DANIEL: Jokes, yeah.

ERIC: Doesn't seem so funny anymore.

DANIEL: You reckon next week we could do some of the applications together?

ERIC: Of course we can.

DANIEL: I'd like that. Nice way to finish up, innit.

ERIC: Just because you don't have to come here because of the terms of your license anymore doesn't mean –

DANIEL: Still trying to *therapise* me, E?

ERIC: You're beyond *therapising*, fam.

DANIEL: Ark at you giving it all the lingo.

ERIC: Both learning.

DANIEL: Yeah. We are.

> **DANIEL** *looks at his watch.*

Time's up.

ERIC: Yeah.

DANIEL: Better be going. Need to change the dressing on this.

ERIC: You gonna be alright?

DANIEL: All the pretty girls like scars.

ERIC: You reckon?

DANIEL: Gotta hope, innit. Ain't got hope, ain't got nothing.

> **DANIEL** *stands and starts towards the door.*

ERIC: I'll see you next week, yeah?

DANIEL: Yeah.

ERIC: I'll print out those job applications.

DANIEL: I'll chore a pen from WH Smiths on the way.

ERIC: I'll provide the pens.

DANIEL: We'll make a youth worker out of you yet.

> **DANIEL** *stops at the door.*

It was that boy's mates. The one who lost his eye. So you ain't got to worry. Promise. It weren't about the strap.

ERIC: Why did they come for you? You weren't the one who –

DANIEL: You don't know me, E. Told you that.

> *A silence.*

ERIC: You've changed.

DANIEL: People don't change. Told you that too.

ERIC: I think you're wrong.

DANIEL: Have to agree to disagree then, won't we?

ERIC: You're not that same kid that sat down in here with me on the first session.

DANIEL: Nah, you've pussied me up.

ERIC: You were always a pussy. You just didn't know it.

> **DANIEL** *suddenly hugs* **ERIC**.

> *It's hard and felt and takes him completely by surprise.*

DANIEL: Thank you. For everything.

He breaks away. Starts towards the exit, stops. Turns back towards **ERIC**.

E…

ERIC: Yeah?

DANIEL: You ever think about the fact this is the only place we get to talk? Not just me and you… Everyone. Everyone in the whole fucking world. So busy with their phones. Their schemes. Trying to make p's… Get laid… Make out they're some big man. This. This is the only fucking place where you can just be you… With none of that out there… None of that shit.

Beat

You ever feel like that, E?

ERIC: Yeah.

DANIEL: Too little, innit.

ERIC: Yeah.

DANIEL: Too late.

A silence.

Laters, yeah.

ERIC: Laters.

DANIEL *exits.*

25.

The same room.

ERIC *lays out some papers on the floor in front of the empty chair opposite him.*

He takes out his vape and smokes.

Rearranges the papers.

He vapes some more.

He checks his watch.

Moves to the door.

Takes out his phone and calls someone. No answer.

He comes back in and sits at his chair again

26.

The same room.

ERIC *sits with his phone in his hand.*

He's crying.

He moves to the empty chair opposite him and hugs it.

27.

The office.

SARA: Communication?

ERIC: Six.

SARA: Working with others?

ERIC: Six.

SARA: Setting and achieving goals?

ERIC: Six.

SARA: Confidence?

ERIC: Six.

SARA: Reliability?

ERIC: Six.

SARA: Leadership skills?

ERIC: Six.

SARA: Managing feelings?

    A silence.

    Managing feelings?

    ERIC *laughs in disgust.*

SARA: It's a simple question.

ERIC: It really isn't.

SARA: Eric…

ERIC: He was doing well.

SARA: Yes, you said. But you have to fill out the paperwork, complete the numerical matrix on the form, or –

ERIC: Or what? What exactly is going to happen?

SARA: The data will be incomplete.

ERIC: You think that matters *now*? Numbers on a fucking spreadsheet?

SARA: Yes. Yes I do.

ERIC: So what? So we can hand them over to the government and they can lie about them in the fucking press to make it sound like they are helping? *They're solving the problem.*

Pause.

SARA: I don't like your tone.

ERIC: I don't like sitting here wasting my fucking time.

SARA: You're not wasting your time.

ERIC: What is this then?

SARA: Procedure.

ERIC: Admin?

SARA: We have to produce data or we risk losing our funding.

ERIC: THEY'RE HUMAN FUCKING BEINGS. You can't break down a human being into a score of one to fucking six.

SARA: You want to write an essay for every answer then? You think that's practical.

ERIC: Ticking boxes. That's all we're doing here.

SARA: We tick a few boxes. They give us some money. Everyone's happy.

ERIC: Not everyone.

A silence.

SARA: Had he mentioned to you any interactions with former associates?

ERIC: *Former associates.*

SARA: Yes.

ERIC: You have no idea what's going on out there, do you?

SARA: Fuck you.

ERIC: You going to put that in your report?

SARA: You think I want to be doing this? You think I don't know how you feel? You think I haven't been through exactly the same thing –

ERIC: Seem to be dealing with it okay.

SARA: Keep going and –

ERIC: And what?

SARA: I'll have no other option than to –

ERIC: Give me a disciplinary? That it? I've overstepped my mark? I've got too involved. Fuck your disciplinaries. If it means saving a life then –

SARA: But you didn't save a life, did you?

Pause.

And that's why we have to go through this. That's duty of care. That's covering our backs. And you might not like it. You might think this is a waste of time. But to be honest I couldn't care less. This is about more than your feelings.

ERIC: If I'd have got him rehomed. Got him out of the area… What's the point? What the point in any of this?

ERIC *breaks down.*

SARA: There's more boys like him. That's the point.

ERIC: And what if it always ends up like this?

SARA: It doesn't. You know that more than most.

Pause.

Did you ever see Daniel outside of your sessions?

ERIC: No.

SARA: You're sure?

ERIC: Of course. Boundaries.

SARA: Good.

SARA *stands, moves to* **ERIC***. Puts a hand on his shoulder.*

Youth work is medicine for a failed society, Eric. And we're short of doctors.

A beat, then she starts to laugh. Bittersweet.

Fuck. I remember when someone said that to me.

ERIC: Yeah?

SARA: Sounded like bollocks then too.

A silence.

I'll see you tomorrow, Eric. Get some rest.

28.

The community centre.

ERIC *sits facing a* **YOUNG MAN***. The* **YOUNG MAN** *has a hoody on with the hood up.*

A long silence.

ERIC: Dizzy or Stormzy?

Pause.

Grime or Bashment?

Pause.

Skepta or Ed Sheeran?

The **YOUNG MAN** *kisses his teeth.*

A noise. Well, now we're getting somewhere.

BLACKOUT.

END OF PLAY.

CPSIA information can be obtained
at www.ICGtesting.com
Printed in the USA
JSHW041034010422
24505JS00005B/33